春节

Customs, Traditions and Landmarks |
Non-Fiction Series

Copyright © 2022 by Level Learning, INC. and Washington Yu Ying PCS™
Original and Edited Text Copyright © 2022 by Washington Yu Ying PCS™

All rights reserved. No part of this book in whole or part may be reproduced without written permission from the publisher.

Published by Level Learning, INC.

Content Contributors:
Washington Yu Ying PCS™
Level Learning - Ya-Ching Chang

Illustrations by: Josh Taira

Leveling classification based on Level Learning standard. For full description, visit www.levellearning.com

ISBN 978-1-64040-013-9
Simplified Chinese Edition

About Level Learning:
Level Learning provides a literacy focused curriculum specifically designed for K-12 Chinese as a Second Language classrooms. Our program offers 20 levels of specific and detailed objectives, leveled texts and passages, mastery-based online assessment, and analytics to enable data-driven instruction. Level Learning reading curriculum for both literature and informational text emphasize grammar and comprehension skills to help teachers develop confident and independent Chinese language readers. The non-fiction series of books are specifically designed to support our informational text course based on multiple national standards. To learn more about our entire offering, visit www.levellearning.com.

About Washington Yu Ying PCS™:
Washington Yu Ying PCS is a Mandarin English dual language immersion International Baccalaureate (IB) World school. Yu Ying's mission is to inspire and prepare young people to create a better world by challenging them to reach their full potential in a nurturing Chinese/English educational environment. Yu Ying's comprehensive IB, dual immersion curriculum equips students with global competencies for success in the real world. As a leader in immersion education, Yu Ying is determined to advance Chinese language programs and global citizenry education by helping other schools create and strengthen their Chinese programs. For more information, email: products@washingtonyuying.org

每年农历正月初一,是中国人的传统节日春节。中国人会怎么庆祝春节呢?

春节前,人们会先把家里打扫干净。这代表旧的一年就要过去了,新的一年要来了。

春节前,全家人会一起去买东西。人们通常会买春联、新衣服、年糕等东西。

过春节的时候，人们把红色的春联贴在门上，穿上新衣服。因为在中国红色代表吉祥和热闹，很多春节的东西都是红色的。

在农历大年三十的晚上,全家人会坐在一起吃晚饭。晚饭通常会有鱼和年糕。

农历正月初一，新的一年开始了。大人会给孩子们红包，红包里有钱。钱的数字通常会有六和八，因为六代表顺利，八代表发财。

新的一年到了,孩子们会放鞭炮。放鞭炮代表吉祥和热闹。

新的一年到了，人们会说吉祥话拜年，比如，恭喜发财，大吉大利！

直到农历正月十五，中国人都会庆祝新年。大家*希望*新的一年有一个好的开始。

Glossary

	Pinyin	English Definition
农历	nóng lì	lunar calendar
传统	chuán tǒng	tradition
节日	jié rì	festival
春节	chūn jié	Chinese New Year
庆祝	qìng zhù	to celebrate
打扫	dǎ sǎo	to sweep
干净	gān jìng	clean
代表	dài biǎo	to represent
旧	jiù	old or former
买	mǎi	to buy
春联	chūn lián	spring couplet
年糕	nián gāo	rice cake
贴	tiē	to stick, to paste
吉祥	jí xiáng	auspicious, lucky
热闹	rè nao	lively

	Pinyin	English Definition
钱	qián	money
数字	shù zì	numbers
顺利	shùn lì	smoothly, favorably
发财	fā cái	to make a fortune
鞭炮	biān pào	firecracker
拜年	bài nián	to pay a new year's visit to friends and family
恭喜发财	gōng xǐ fā cái	Wishing you a prosperous New Year!
大吉大利	dà jí dà lì	good luck and great profit
希望	xī wàng	to hope

www.ingramcontent.com/pod-product-compliance
Lightning Source LLC
Chambersburg PA
CBHW041223070526
44584CB00001B/63